T0326812

Abrupt Rural

David Dodd Lee

New Issues Poetry & Prose

A Green Rose Book

New Issues Poetry & Prose
The College of Arts and Sciences
Western Michigan University
Kalamazoo, Michigan 49008

An Inland Seas Poetry Book

 Inland Seas poetry books are supported by a grant from
The Michigan Council for Arts and Cultural Affairs.

First Edition, 2004.

ISBN   1-930974-38-8 (paperbound)

Library of Congress Cataloging-in-Publication Data:
Lee, David Dodd
Abrupt Rural/David Dodd Lee
Library of Congress Control Number: 2003113937

Editors   Herbert Scott, Jonathan Pugh

Art Director   Tricia Hennessy
Production Manager   Paul Sizer
                                The Design Center, Department of Art
                                College of Fine Arts
                                Western Michigan University

Abrupt Rural

David Dodd Lee

New Issues

WESTERN MICHIGAN UNIVERSITY

Also by David Dodd Lee

Contents

Color, Eyelids of

All's light at

eye level

the cold the lull

your body relaxes into

not momentary blindness

but darkness

upon which for a few seconds

a willed nothing

turns into something

only the insides of the eyelids, perhaps

or simply *not light,* as Parmenides said it

not light but thought blooming

the idea of yellow

lit up like a lodestar

for instance

whatever you choose to make it

Offspring, Once Removed

Thinking too hard, you can lose it,
easily. Harder to lose embossed documents,
although you wish sometimes you could

walk nameless through the goldenrod to the glade

where the willow shades on the other side
of the silver pond,
a fresh shovel and a hole in the ground.

Dignified, like a man with a grand piano he has to give up.
Like a huddle of horses steaming in a field.

Everyone frowns and goes home.

Somebody's son sticks his finger inside
a shotgun shell and gets bitten by a spider.

The kid's face is slapped
and the shell settles upright on the shoulder
of a well-traveled road.
It fills with rain. Fat chance he's heading for a winning hand.

A birth certificate trembles in its plastic sleeve.

In the Black Kitchen

It begins early, arc crumbling over the yard with its salt bird baths.
Then you dream of the banister gleaming, your hand
from atop the stairs gripping a tiny casket. Heat gathers above the
    local graveyard
that dusts so resolutely the young men's shoes with its flags.
This is where the shadows meet the white wall. Since
you were a boy you've moved unmolested right through them.
But you are never alone. You are never without the crumbs
your father scraped off your black toast. The whiter the appliance
the rounder its corners. The reflections on the floor are cut into many
    small pieces.
There's nowhere to hide. He keeps looking in the window at you.

New Smell

During the blackout, she's under the lightbulb.
Without function, it becomes something else in her sphere, a sculpture
beyond which the lakeshore runs like a Cristo of wrack and dead fish.
Dear lonely poet, please don't knock. Leave a note on the door.
She has shredded the only small book of verse I ever brought home
saying she wants what's immediate, skinless.
In the meantime, this range of tender avoidances.
Yet her hair spills like silk over the new berber, a tessellation of
    suicidal intentions and dry goods.

No Good

I'm sick of Edward Hopper and his nostalgia for light.

Let it be other than fragile,
The way time denies memory a clear visual shape, pure blur.

Her face is no longer even in reach.

Distance or not, what is she when she turns away to pick up
   her toothbrush . . .

Some of what we know we can know only with our hands.

And what about the way the light of the instant ricochets off the backs of
   her knees.

It keeps shifting.

It needs to be stilled.

Instead of a Father

Because the mind conceives a love of its own,
and because it places this love,

because the hands fall in a radiating numbness outside the mind's hunger,
because love in fact drips from the mind's eaves

instead of a father, instead of a ribbon flying out of a grave,
instead of a handful of corn, instead of a crucifix,

I crave sleep and dream. I wake and we make love.
Because the mind conceives a love,

because I have married some father's daughter, because my daughter
    drowned
in her parent's vast masonry, because I left matters pending but often
    shouldn't have.

I wake and we don't make love. Last night she said *How sad to be dead
and have no one who could write your biography.* No friends, family.
    Because wind

driving sleet through the mind is what I was thinking. Because I was
    startled
awake. Because the pasture of torches burns a hole

in the midnight of weather. Because the past must stand before the
    mind now.
Because the mind conceives a love instead of the father.

Nothing But Dust

The old men have drunk their fill.
A few glasses litter the room. A ceiling fan spins.
When the heavy door swings open
the light that pours into the room reveals dust

on some of the bottles behind the bar.
Out front a dirty white mongrel with pointed ears

sits watching the men fish for their keys.
They all get into their trucks to drive home.
The bartender picks up the glasses,

four to a hand, and sets them upside-down in the glass washer.
She wipes down the tables with a damp cloth.
The dog looks both ways and crosses the street.

A man pulls into the lot.
It's been dry. The dust never settles.
The waitress brings him a glass of ice water.
She hands him a plastic menu.

He rubs the back of his neck with his hand.
He puts his arms on the bar. The bartender is reading a seed catalogue.
He wants a Dead Mariner.

She begins mixing the drink in one of those steel shakers.
His hands are trembling,
dirt under his fingernails.
Three o'clock in the afternoon and he's still not hungry.

Stone Effigy

A stone told me *You'll soon be leaving us*
What about my sister?
The stone told me *No, your sister's a spider*

*

I lived with a rock garden under a palm tree,
built a wall some years later around my small slate house
in its nice bowl of a valley . . .

Portland cement and creek limestone
sealed off the other side . . .

The simple tap of a hammer, halving the bluestone,
a weightlessness, like a sudden absence of pain . . .

*

There are things
I wish I could talk
about among the others
stones or bottle-nosed dolphins not exactly the point

fin cutting the silken waters
to ribbons   a pelican stroking a wake across
a ferromanganese sky—

That's not even close

*

how the stars pull them out of their rooms

how the woman is naked, her head placed inside a noose
by her younger brother

how her hair pours over his wrist like blood

how the dented moon, a faraway rock, shines on the small
gray house

how she kisses his cheek with a second rope

how there's a sound like stone gears
grinding out dust

how the spider runs through the open front door into moonlight

how the hangings take place

how the smell of the sea continues to drift through the windows
and into the silent house

Hickory Corners

I remember the piece of twine, how it dangled from a hole
in his boot. More hours drunk, and never mind
how hard you shook him. His eyes wandered
like desert birds while the room pivoted under the sun, the only sound
the ticking of his enormous watch. *Father, here are the photos*
of your childhood, in this shoebox.
I am going to place them in the furnace.
Instead I hid them in a wind nursery under the porch.
He used to produce coins out of my ear. Once, while he slept
in a slurry of vomit, I stole the watch. I buried it.
I spent the next week sleeping in the barn with the horses.

Curvature of the Spine

It wasn't all that long ago I watched a guy drink himself
to death he really died pissed all over himself first   all over
  the couch
later I saw the boxcutter in the sink   I wish I could have saved him
that same week I saw a giant swallowtail come up from Florida
  banking like
a boat through the Dakota-like plains west of Galesburg
and knew I was a little bit singing / dying each minute
  my hands
clutching the wheel of the mower   she was the angel of death
  that butterfly
And then my hands on the girl   who dreamed and dreamed
  while I kissed her
I watched her circulate in her clothes   Then I started thinking
I'm not capable of thinking   I'm just beating the wind with my nuts
I tell you from there things get foggy   like many arrows whistling
through rain   a confluence of vanishing points   As a child I lived
  near a hollow
scooped out in the dunes   I watched the dying alewives float
  through
my armpits   their eyes sealed tight as iron
my spine grew about as straight as a grapevine strangling a
  phone pole
As long as I can remember the trees have always clung to the cliffs
  of sand
Nothing begins with me   Nothing stays the same   Nothing gropes
  its way home
Those days and now These   snapdragons and morning glories
marigolds   I ate a basket of purple beans last night   grew them in
  the damp arbor
sun of the late afternoons   when you throw them in boiling water
  they turn green
it's a miracle of alchemy   they were still crunchy because I was so
  hungry
I went to buy my girlfriend a goldfish   I think of small bass shifting
over a moonlit bed   I think of hot water cutting grease off a knife
I clotheslined this guy one time   he was holding a coffee cup full of
  beer

it was a long time ago   there was an old wood stove smoking in the
   corner
of a room   it was full of burning hickory
the ground outside was littered with fresh dogwood petals
I reached my fingers out for a second because I thought it was
   snowing
I left the fish in its bag   he didn't die but almost   I opened the door
   to her trailer
Tom   she said   Rick?   the TV was going
she was watching a show about weather
all I could see was a shutter torn off a house and blown
across an empty street   she had one lamp on   I got out
of there quickly   I started thinking about my life   the way it
   sometimes
sparkled like a bluegill caught in the sun or grew dark
like the rain in a yard full of lumber and bricks   I could see my
   breath
I peed off a culvert   I listened to the hum of a streetlight
it kept getting later and later   I walked all night
At dawn I saw that giant swallowtail slowly fanning her black wings
in my driveway like a candle burning inside an empty church

Beauty of Women

1.
There are many places to go, and in all of them someone is going to die.

Along the Thornapple River once
I found the body of a woman floating
Inside a froth of twigs and fishline.

She didn't smell like pine trees, but the air did . . .

I gripped a big birch tree and brushed her
With a giant spruce bough

The wind threw hooks through. Sometimes I wake in bed
    right when my body
Sloughs one old bag of skin for another. My hands, sometimes,
Are only matter-shaped-into-hands.

2.
Hidden estuary, a bell in the fog,
Smoky harmonics
Drifting north out of the Saginaw smog . . .

I fell asleep right while I was looking at her.

Woman of the eighty brailles of bark
Woman of the dead night herons
            Woman of the shovel
And wheelbarrow of fish
Woman of the railroad and creosote and insect vibrations
Woman of the converging two-tracks heading north
through a harbor of firs with their heads boughed
Woman of the tongue and the groove
Woman of the 8,000 bunkbeds
Woman of snow filling the bell of a wine glass
Woman of the moon watching you sleep after midnight

3.
What should a dying woman do?
Bodiless, she'll have given up everything to leave us
(She'll have given up nothing) . . .

4.
I'd like to ruin the beauty of women, or

Embrace it, embrace death. That day, I had one brown trout
Nested on mint grass inside my creel, fish soft and white as fresh
    snow.
The eyes moved—the bottomless eyes—when I stroked
The trout's belly.

5.
I used to let myself sink to the floor of Lake Michigan,
Holding my knees in tight. I'd rock slightly under the small waves.

Soon, I'd think, *a child is going to be born.*

Lake Winnipeg

Dark
like an animal's fur, dew-covered, a little oily
as if decay might be arrested

Night
or nurtured, loved. Then blood on a single leaf,
curled near a hatchet,
a bag full of feet
under an almost-full moon.
Although this harbor's full moon lacks a sliver

Animal
of love. A marten, on hunt, creeps from behind the boathouse,
its teeth shining like lemons.

Bones
The man sees them in the dark, turns up the lamps via rheostat.
Someone else wakes,
thinking *butchered,* thinking

Trees
okay so he's upset. This happens on the other side
of the lake,
trees crowding the skinny peninsula,

Johnboat
turning evanescent the image of the flowers left
standing on the dock
in the mist of twilight. She feels an ache
in her teeth where she's been biting splitshot,
pike blood deep in her nails.
He'd drive a chisel into the fishes' brains,
and now her iron's fucked up. Nothing's true north.
    She's cold

Fillet Knife
and frightened. And a muskrat dives, comes up gleaming. But on-
ly the animal sees it.

A Story About Ice

I might as well admit it: I am frightened of ice, the way
it begins as a tiny flame—invisible, really—& then grows
into an icicle as water rinses over itself. I sleep while this goes on,
    I cook dinner,
maybe watch TV. Outside the sparrows
multiply, & sometimes dodge away from their reflections. My neighbor,
after taking out her garbage,
walks with her hands in her pockets, reflected upside-down in ice,
    her breath
small puffs of exhaust she chugs away from . . .

And I am frightened of the lathered knobs & swells of ice
on Lake Michigan, on which snow continues to fall even while one is
dreaming of a child who has drowned.
The snow falls and falls. And it sings while it falls, a song
like the sadness of those still living, consoling each other, or praying.
The drowned child floats now, & the sun has managed to spring loose,
a lion of a sun
melting a little the clear, unconscious ice resting under the weight
    of the atmosphere.
The child—a boy—is on a raft with a blue bedspread tucked in
    over its corners.
He is drifting. He has been drifting for a while, over deeper & deeper
    water.

    *

Nothing stays the same. By January the earth has tilted away from
    the sun.
Sparrows huddle near the wrists of knotted wood
deep inside a shrub that has been pruned into a perfect cube.
What I mean is there is not always this fear.
                       The water rushes back & forth
under Muskegon Lake's flat ice. And the weeds down there
wave in the current. A teardrop swings like a dead boy
riding the moon on a string & a small yellow fish feels something—
I guess it would be stupid to call it happiness—

and she presses her lips against the blue teardrop
and inhales it & even thinks she may now go rest

in her place beside several brown rocks
where the paper mill pours warm water into a cove after cooling
the huge machines that flatten & cook & dry the industrial-sized
    sheets of paper.

There is a man whose job it is to keep the roof clear of ice at the
    paper mill.
He looks around a giant vent pipe at the lake while he tosses salt
from bags attached to his belt. He moves his feet on the delicate
rung of the ladder, which vibrates
from the constantly moving gears inside the plant.

    *

Anyway, the fish, a perch, has been hooked
and so she's not going anywhere except up toward the circle of light
that hovers overhead like the quietest ringing,
something we all hear as long as we're alive, like a finger pressed
    to our foreheads.

Maybe the ringing, once we're dead, grows louder, like a siren.
But as we leave the flesh it fades away like a bird flying off
    a telephone
wire & disappearing inside a dense patch of woods . . .

The boy on his blue raft is singing now, inside the fish's mouth.
He is drowned forever. Which is why his raft is blue, the color of
a summer sky, the color of his mother's eyes.

                    And the perch is *flipped*
onto the ice, which is safe for now, holding us all up. And she has
    brought some dark green
weeds with her, laced through her gills, & the weeds stripe the snow
and scatter in small dark flecks like a bright constellation
she stretches across the middle of, gasping for breath.

    *

There is nothing to fear. I have fallen through ice
and I did not die. I have traveled in my car that is like its own

private galaxy
and have felt it veer off through the universe on sheets of black ice—

So this is what death will be like, I may have thought.

Like a man on a ladder, a little unsteady when
a wasp flies too close, like the boy
waking from a dream
about canoeing a smooth cold river but who instead finds himself
   swallowing water
in his room. After a while he gives in & relaxes & breathes & goes
   back to sleep
and dreams once again of the small window above his bed
streaming and shiny from a silver midsummer rain.

The Quarry

None of us has a clue
how the owls know what to whisper to the deer,
leading them into water.
The deer around Cold Station have been fighting
a disease which robs them of memory.
Eventually they go blind.
That's when the screech owls ride them,
pick out the nameless red ticks the deer
have been carrying,
the cause of their illness.
The tick has a white circle
on its abdomen—like a target—
and the ability to fly.
Once the disease has progressed
to the point where a deer
can no longer remember,
once its eyes have turned white,
the owl leads it to the quarry,
coos in its ear
directions to the blast-holes full of still water.
On any given Saturday you can
drive down Van Buren and see the birds aloft
over the ponds, circling,
looking down. Sometimes they line
the top of the cliff,
fifteen or twenty of them,
their feathers riffling in the wind,
wondering what to do next.

Fall Again

1.
There's too much to think about.
Somebody explain.

Forget it, don't anyone speak . . .

Feel your lover's pulse for a second instead.

Fast-forward to the day of your death:
Is she there
beside your bed? Has everything coalesced
in such a way
in your imagination as to make passage
into the next world a glorious event?

Let it all fall down around your feet,
simple as the loose threads
you've clipped with nail clippers off the seams of your
    sad blue sweatshirt.

Why is it sad?
Everyone's got one, even the rich,
who go on talking and talking
under the burnished light that arrests time,
or seems to.

Why don't you smoke a few cigarettes and think about it for a while.

The blue sweatshirt and why it is so terribly sad.

                    From the very beginning we grow
large inside our clothes,
and shed them occasionally.
Where are they all now?

When a loved one dies
somebody has to empty the closets, sort through the piles
heaped onto a bed— . . .

A woman picks up the phone, dials half a number,
and replaces the receiver.

2.
Nobody cares, particularly, about my grief.

Is there a philosophy book I should read?
There are always the photographs, shining behind plastic.

Aim, shoot, print: ten years later
                              one still can't
copulate with a memory.

We were young once and it was spring.
Sperm drifted to the top of the water between us in the cool lake
like a beautiful bird, fluttering close . . .

Wasn't it because we were together that the sun shone down on us . . .

Then an emptiness followed,
burning up in the heat, the sand and lawns turning white
in the distance.

Now it is fall, the beautiful season.
The moon rises over the sickle-shaped
whir of a combine
edging toward chaos in a cornfield near Asylum Lake
like a cast-off sweatshirt's pale
blue unravelling.

Indian Summer

1.
I guess the moon replaces
the deer, or the fish, a little off-register now,
fish with their guts spilling,
dead fish, fish watching.
Unless it replaces the girl. Tracy.

Not Hawkins
                    or the drunk kid crying on the shoulder of the road,
muttering to himself.
Certainly not Wilkinson.
The deer ran in a circle with one eye-
ball rolling around
on its cheek bone. There were autumnal
spirits diving in and out of the

Northern Lights,
that beautiful silence
banging around inside the cavernous cello
of the valley we were stranded in,
the smell of pines heavy in the air. The deer
fell down. Now he was simply bleeding
to death in the middle of the road, while our car
hissed, propped up on a mailbox post,
one headlight shining out into the woods . . .

When the ambulances and cops arrived
I hung back in a shadow that, like a voice,
seemed to speak for me . . .

2.
Because it was the deer who labored for breath,
the only real patient,
the paramedics were pacing with no one to use a stethoscope on.

And suddenly I felt what I can only explain
as a glucose high, watching the steam
rise from the deer's torn body,
while Tracy cried on Wilkinson's shoulder,
his creepy fingers moving around in her hair.
She'd been laughing at his jokes

all day. The fish we'd caught
had somehow stacked themselves up along the street
like sandbags. Suckers, mostly,
many of them still alive.
But some had been split in half
when the pick-up
removed the top of our trunk, and now the separate
halves seemed to *grand-mal*
amidst the calmer stacks of whole fish,
which seemed at peace, mere spectators.

Finally, one of the policemen pulled out a gun.
Even the sobbing drunk turned to watch.
By now the deer had wriggled
its way to the bottom of the ditch.
I began walking the six miles
back to the cabin. I thought of the season as I walked.

October, and warm.

Indian summer.

Pregnant moon fat as a pig in the sky.

I was feeling better. The young cop, in his nervousness,
had started counting down at ten.
So I was well on my way when I heard
the shots. Two close together.
And then the third, the finishing off.

The New Alphabet

It may be time lies down. As if at the center
stillness of an enormous flower—octagonally spoked
with various ways out—before drying up,
the way memory fades, the way we become not who we were
but are, dead-centered, yellow as pollen or gray
as the charred stone
of earthly caves we become an axis of,
the broken hands of a clock, the blare of the television
threatening to drown us as the seconds slide by . . .

*

All necessary,
the true or false impression
breathing creates—the stars' bright burning,
which, as soon as we close our eyes,
reappears. Roar like a train reverberating
inside a tunnel, pliers
of anti-gravity, rust falling off the radio flyer, a convicted rapist
plucking petals from the eye of a sawdust-stuffed womb,
round and hot as the mind's
black sun . . .

*

Okay, I'm elsewhere, uninvolved: emotionally limited.
But forget about that: diesel fuel ignites
the snowy explosion of stamen and pistil.

One can make of this what one wants. I can hold out my hand
    for a century
until my nails become carbon, sprinkled with nuclear dust.

My heart trips like a staple gun, eye on the cursor,
until the satellite feed in the phone lines ignites, flares like phospher,
burns up . . .

*

Our lives are short. The lives of the people we decide
to love are short. My daughter's cantering horse

swings into the blazing orbit
of the speedier tilt-a-whirl, up over the bulbs flashing
Elephant Ears. Then she's smoking a cigarette
under a willow, grown tall and serious.

Whole constellations dry up in the time it takes for me to
    feel comfortable with her again,
although I can E-MAIL her in a matter of seconds.

*

The minute hand whirls noisily around
like the train clattering by on the L, green words
shaken out of a blue sentence,
your old typewriter's platen begging to be sucked off,
small and abstract, lovely as a river of Xes or ampersands,
the whirr of a cartridge clicking into place,
a stampede of copies,
a new alphabet.

Beauty

It could be enough, a little light through the leaves, clouds reflecting off
   water
while I eat an orange, a nap in the afternoon, the sun warm
on my back, long long hours just thinking. I'm my father's
son, that's for sure, intolerant, but lonely, disarmed
by the problem of living completely inside myself.
My lover's across town, in her bed. We fucked all afternoon,
then I drove home to avoid having to talk to her kid,
just three and a half, who'd be back from his father's, and watching
   cartoons.
He's a hyper little guy, admittedly cute, likes to hang from my belt
while I spin. We pretend he's a plane, something I never did,
play with adults, since I was taught to sit still and watch.
That was a long time ago. And I became good at what I was taught.
Too good, I guess, bright water, the trees, her hair lifting in a warm
   breeze.
She's home with her son. It's sunny. He's nothing like me.

Her Body

I love how her body closes its eyes when she begins to come.

The black pond drinks in the red birds.

The spiders suddenly grow enormous in their dew-soaked webs.

Last year's brown, curled leaves blow simultaneously across all the highways.

The owl hears the rabbit's heartbeat from a branch in a tall white pine.

The leaves on the maples grow violently still before a thunderstorm.

A bell has been struck by a raindrop.

Pulse

Like the wing of a butterfly there was the river

that walked every night there was the blood in your wrist
the window and the solitary white pine in the rain

there was the white bird

there were seeds in a soup can and the bag of potatoes
a black widow dangling in her web between the used-up brooms

there was the man holding his hat in his hands
looking for the cemetery

there was the dog crossing the cornfield
a pile of stumps burning in a ditch by the side of the road

in the middle of the night
an apple core drying in the breezeway

a dinner bell rings far off
an owl flies out the barn door

Two Strangers

1.
My sister used to sing the *Scissors Song* from her crib.
I'd dream she was dead, just another sleeping insect,
cicada unable to close its eyes.

2.
It's just the moon, my mother said late one night, sitting on my bed,
   making shadows.

3.
White birds dipped in candle wax hung upside-down in the closet.
Cats with no hair on their heads looked in through the windows.

My father grew from a small boy into an adult
in the corner. I could never sleep.

4.
I was afraid of the light coming in through the keyhole.

Once I looked through it. Saw two strangers. A man and a girl.
The man was trying to braid the girl's hair while she wept.

Duplicate Trigger

All the clothes in the world, and no homes. Now, nearly evening,
   Lola yawns,
stands blinking in the narrow hallway . . .

I pick up the serrated knife and slice the beef and it runs
clear and pink.

Steam rises in a cloud as if out of the body of a still-living priest.

God, using the throat of a mockingbird, slips in a musical phrase
that could be an old churchyard gate
slowly closing. I know then the boy is gone,

and I have to wonder if he ever really existed.
Sometimes I ask Lola real questions. "Do you want to walk
around in the field on the other side of the highway and look for bottles?"

"May I fix you a grilled-cheese sandwich?"

I love it when she crosses her lips with her thumb after prayer,

in the name of Saint Luke.

"I'm going to take his clothes to the river. I don't think anyone else
should have them. Will you come with me? Just nod. I don't want to hear
   you speak."

Dry Creek Bed

I look down at the rain that is filling this ditch
where formerly I wished to lie down in the grass and sleep

under a withering of leaves, right through the coming winter
and beyond, an exhilaration of fresh blood filling my skull

with the incalculable romance of life, my beautiful life
filling this bed with the incomparable waters of death.

Pressing Down

In the small two-room treehouse I grew up in
you can look down onto the lights reflecting
off the bowl of Cold Station Lake.

Blurred milk of stars printed on water, a few houses
hidden under cover of birch trees and firs.

Sometimes I read a book by candlelight just to make life a little cozier.

My parents drowned themselves here.

They live deep in the forest now.

Sometimes I hear them moving through the woods, but mostly they sleep.
For so long that's all they wanted to do.

At night the deep water stands perfectly still.

The Trays Near the Sinks

And then we couldn't. The drain was a suit dyed
black, one foot dreaming in a cave.

That's why we never slept, martyrs
posing from different parts of the stage.

She moistened his knees.
He sharpened the blade.

A dragonfly sewed the kindling of the dead
sister into the ground with carpet thread.

That's one place to go.

A little speed with your strychnine.
Eyes closed but dilated.

She placed one hand on the back of my neck
and the turquoise water rippled, susurrations of dreams . . .

Black shoes, your vase was mysteriously empty.
Wide open, but humming. By noon we'd surrendered.

My Little Hard Time

Flower—a blind man's word.
                    —Paul Celan

Jail time, less time. I spent two nights in jail
on the steel slab provided for me.

Jail is 98% shadow, 2% light.

Those crybabies on the outside, complaining about the cold weather . . .

*

Less time in the sun, less time with a woman, less time reading poems
at an Independent Bookstore near me.

A guy with his eye swelled shut
said to no one in particular:
"It's amazing how much this place resembles a toilet, and I'm not
speaking metaphorically."

The phone I eventually used was like picking up an ice-cold barbell.

They bring you potatoes with gravy & meat ground up
to resemble particle board, a sodium & carbohydrate cocktail
for breakfast.

*

When you wade into a river
it is not like jail. Emerson's transparent eyeball
is not dilated in jail. There is a kind of mist
in jail, but it is complete. God is not
hiding in the mist. Your parents
are not hiding in the mist.
Your lover is not hid-
ing in the mist.

It is not nature-made. *No bones of the past.* No past.

Gardening and Government

1.
It's not because you're desperate for a job
Lansing passes a resolution against
"produce freshening by hand."

Oranges and limes and that little sprayer
thing with the cold mist.
A mechanical mister, then.

As soon as this becomes law
all the degreed gardeners with their heads down journaling
stop. Begin weeding, pruning, grumbling.

2.
The sun shines the same as it did when you were
holding court with your glass
of icy bourbon, pondside . . .

Dear Harbor of the Black Rooms where the Fish
Speak in Low Tones

about the Development of an Anti-Fileting Machine . . .
a female fish has disrobed.
Ah, so might you, had you such cold lips.

The former Governor
of the great state of Michigan still sometimes wakes feeling alarmed.
Afraid his actual flesh

is expanding, almost touching the Indiana border, in essence
touching a Hoosier.

Dressed in a synthetic body suit and tails,
he lets the help freshen his drink to the sound of conversion
taking place in the plush leaves overhead.

The Glacial Recession North
or Following the Money Home

Loneliness, the crumbling edge of a Midwestern city. Love, and its
cousin, depravity.

Southwest of Indianapolis, a wall, or a scrim of dust.
It chops the hillier land and those people away.
There's safe passage into Ohio. Then north.
I remember the heat like a wave, the yeasty smell of the
Mississippi River . . .

Red plastic cups slosh in the foam. Love, and its cousin,
my parents.

My parents and their odd relationship to each other.

Depravity,
the whole lot of us scratching our ankles
and waiting
for the patriarch to show up.

Somebody suggests revising the fine fine parchment of our
family history while we wait to flee to Michigan . . .

My mother, and her cousin, loneliness. Her estrangement
and love of the steely blue vastness of the hostile north.

The people in northern Indiana could only
brush the sand from their corduroy vests
and check through the back sliding doors the condition
of their goldfish ponds and bird feeders . . .

My father, the dead with their clipboards and Federal Bureau of
　　Investigation sunglasses.
My mother, the absolutely angelic
waiters at the Dunes du Lac in the uniform of pallbearers . . .

A Little Night

Nobody in the group outside Whippi-Dip
Understands if it's the crushing cold of ice cream
Bunching around tense molars
That's playing havoc with moods
Or simply the effect of a dark bank of clouds having just rolled in.

The youngest, a boy, says "I'm cold" but he is underheard.
The two blonde sisters sit down next to each other
So they can argue over who stole whose lipstick.

As a shadow crosses the small carved-up table, pupils dilate. They all
React to this. The mother feels a tingling in her groin and looks
At her husband. She feels this in her breasts. Her libido
Surges from the change of light, temperature.

The sisters lapse into dreaming about the past. Both
Of them sail over some nearby firs. And the father considers buying a
   beef barbecue, he is
Suddenly so starving. A different girl, some kid,
Having just arrived on her bike, sits a few tables away. She watches
   the leaves as the wind rises
Flapping the Hawaiian-print shirt against the starving man's back.

She loves the weather: *When isobars arrange themselves*
Tightly around a low pressure center
They form a kind of valley for the wind to plunge into. The tighter
The pattern, the faster the wind rushes into the hole
like water down a steep grade, runoff pooling into a river or a lake.

The girl gets all goosepimply recalling this metaphor,
Compliments of a happy-seeming black man on The Weather Channel.

"It feels like it's already night," the woman says, and tongues
The sharp tip of her sugar cone. "A little night in the middle of day."

"I'm still hungry," the father says, missing his wife's meaning.

The boy feels his family all around him, closer now, closer
Than is welcome—the dry, dry skin, the exultant breathing. He looks at
the solitary Girl swinging her legs beneath the picnic table bench.

The wind blows. The temperature keeps dropping.

Now she is putting down her white plastic spoon.
Now she is taking off her glasses.
Now she is brushing her hair up around her small ears and watching
the trees.

His breath catches . . .

He wonders what it would feel like to freeze to death.

The Pasture

—Borgess Medical Center, Kalamazoo, Michigan

1.
Troubling, the dark clouds passing, gravid with hidden light.
Some melting on the other side of the pasture. Out here,
Where something like water dripping from blue leaves counts as a
    cardiovascular event.

2.
Cut to *Diabetes*. At the hospital
The humming
In the dialysis room and the bruised yellow skin and the smell.
    Bulbs, swarms of insects
Whose eyes insinuate . . .
Forever's foreshadowing—an eternity of nights—followed
    by sparks skidding off a tray of needles . . .

A patient once told me, in a sweat, that he was going to drown in
    a flood.
I saw no water.
But it could have been the simple flickering of the fluorescent lights . . .
"And it's so goddamned hot in this fucking movie," he said.

3.
Sometimes I put my face in the water. I don't cup it, demurely,
    and drink
Or wash. I open my eyes in the creek.
I never see much. The water's too cold. The part of my face dipped
Into the creek freezes.

A ring of white, like paint, frozen marbles for eyes.
Immediately afterwards I'm blind. I can't see my hands. I can't see
The water that is running down my arms, but I can feel it.

4.
I push my cart into the room. Diabetes exacerbated by alcoholism.
His fingers are gangrenous. While the machine works on his kidneys
His dessicated hands

Remain hooked in the air, like claws.
I stuff bags of normal saline into slots, primary and secondary tubing,
Pour hundreds of plastic syringes into metal baskets.

What do they do with the fingernails once they fall off?

5.
From the shade of cottonwoods I watch a cow piss on its calf.

People I've memorized, memories I've embellished—they all begin
    talking to each other
In some corner of the pasture, under a lavender tent, that golden drizzle.

Sometimes death smells like rain, the first dust-raising drops,
Sometimes like the too-clean rape of medical cleaning fluids.

That man and his fingers, my ex-wife, scare me. The woman crying
    into her hatbox in the parking garage
Scares me. Sometimes a stroll through 3/NorthWest feels like an
    inundation of gnats.

The photo of a sunset moves across the wall, light filtering through a tree.

A fax machine grinds out a piece of graph paper,
The words to a song near a sketch of a daisy . . .

There's obviously more than just us.

But mostly lights blink.

6.
The cows across the street, many of which are being sucked dry, cry out
    in pain
Or ecstasy, who can tell. They're gazing skyward,
The front of each face ringed by the warm paint of what's next.

The Mailbox on Parkview

I'm afraid when I die
it will be to take up residence
in an empty grave
full of wind & the reverberating
sounds of settling,
like a house seconds before the wrecking
    ball,
but not nearly as much fun.

Have you ever wondered, as you stand on a curb
holding a letter, waiting
for the traffic to clear,
if anyone sees you at all,
& how maybe it's better that nobody does, given
the misrepresentation
of the homely flesh
that grips too tightly the thin white envelope
that will soon be given over
to more careless manipulations
than you'd care to think about
on its way to some loved one?

After ten years
probably the basic pine casket develops a few cracks.
The pale thunk of a yellow grub.
It moves its bullet head
toward your bones, leaving an invisible trail
of protective mucus
that would shine in the daylight,
that would beautifully scar
a flat piece of paper.
It rests in the peat
of your skull for a month.

Paper is so dry, human beings, eventually
    dry.
It's time to cross the road.

Re: Plant Food. Does anyone else see this?
With the most delicate care

I have selected a typeface with fine
sloping serifs
& dropped the envelope face-up
into the darkness of a domed blue mailbox,
where it sits with the others,
the dead, soon to be reborn, a gasp
like a too-long-held exhalation.

I prefer it this way. My Love to You.

Rural Route

—Pup Creek Falls, Marquette County

We could end up that far north.
I thought about this while shaving,
First the menthol cream heaped
Like snow on a branch, poised on the tips

Of three fingers. It's cold, scraping the foam off,
Erasing the black stubs
(that forest of stumps), while her neck grows long
in the mirror as the drift of her body entire.

I'm washing her hair during Indian summer,
Soap on her shoulders. When I remove the towels
I start shaving hair from her legs
And she shivers. Love, it's so cold up here.

The doe about to drink breathes on the river.
She kneels on a bed
Of green moss, picks up the razor. It's freezing,
This shave. Steam floats over the water,

Acidic with tannin.
And an owl perches on a branch,
Her head turning out of the wind.
When she's finished we nap among pines,

Everything bright, chalk of a quarter moon.
Our new mailbox gleams, filled with catalogues,
Then tips over. Pine boughs move in the wind,
While the deer, her silence nearly human,

Leaps through a ravine that leads nowhere,
Or as far as the owl can see,
Who's been watching us inside her theater of interest,
The light crashing down all around her.

July Garden

1.
Delirious, or one might say *cutaneously*
sublime, the soft soft flowers like clouds or feathers . . .
One could certainly say *sexual*—the way the garden hose
pours its cold heart into mulch . . .

Have you noticed how the leaves
in this flowerbed jostle, fight to touch one another
in the slightest hot breeze?

It's arousing to watch.

Light flickers through the crimson maple,
dusting the peonies'

bright red blossoms, one of which my friend's child plucks
and chews. Do we all think the same words?:

"Noah is eating a flower." Maybe, but his mother says "Thorns!"
But there are no thorns, just petals.

It's sunny out, and the teenaged kid across the street has arrived
home with a busted-out windshield.

Just petals . . .

2.
A house finch meets a goldfinch underneath an oriole nest
and they waltz, spin off. As we move through the garden a variegated
    hydrangea eventually
covers the boy,
who is still eating his flower in the shade.

The buoyed-up blossoms of nearby phlox bob as if floating on water.
A breeze slinks out of the buzz of distant traffic, creeps through the valley.

Our roses are pink, yellow. Peace Roses.

3.
A woman fills a hypodermic and her skin flushes around
a subcutaneous prick. Her angel, who is in heaven, undresses
and sleeps surrounded by roses.

Bed of thorns she dreams in.

Orgasm of flesh dimpling.

Moss flowing over ticking bones
like collapsing water.

A minuscule red blossom appears
on pale skin.

Noah is eating a flower.

April

The child swims out of my body. Deep under the ground
the remaining children swim out of my father's body,
a thousand blue tears, among the calcified stars.

My father swims out of his body.

He cries like a lost child under the web of stars.

The child swims out of my body, a star,
and through the columns of shade pouring down
   out of the universe.

Ishpeming

—The dead are perfectly preserved
in the ice-cold Superior water

So the hardware store in town shuts down

It isn't late   it's winter

Lake Superior hums like a mountain range   it's always that deep . . .

The girl's drowned sister sleeps in its water

Dimly, she is a mirror

Dark in the morning   Dark in the evening

The giant furnace at the hardware store whooshes on

The girl switches off her lights

She adjusts her radio   tuned to the sound

Of snow falling

She is conscious of the shape of her face

She listens in the dark

The snow unfolding—an animal turning around in her room

Village After This One

I love you, world, despite my incommensurate
lack of confidence in your keeping on:
the street blowing with spits of snow
turns like a page I might doom
to darkness after reading it, forever,
or until I reopen the book. Then:
there it is, sun filtering
through the air
like faerie dust
raining down as I turn out of the dark isthmus
laid down by a basswood.
Okay. How to proceed
from here: I open the book
and see a thousand black shapes
like birds slowly coming into focus
over a marsh on a windy fall day.
I close the book, or look
away. Happiness, you are only memory
sometimes. But you will die full
of the light that troubles your precious
sadness. Be glad for once.

Unrecordable

—Pike Lake, Michigan, Upper Peninsula

The phone booth leans under the boughs of a lightning-sheared
maple photographed while the car creeps warmly forward

in the thrall of a long grass belly-rub; a dragonfly with a white eyespot
quivering on its split tail rides the antenna for a blink
then banks supersonically into these woods no one's ever hiked through.

The land sometimes scribbles its own name.
I carry a camera instead of a notebook.

It's not really life in the country. The telephone works.
But the only visible dwellings are two outhouses.
I go inside and photograph the toilet paper

bolted to the wall and padlocked. Nearby, a white-capping lake bouys
a pair of loons, ladderbacked, with flat serpent heads, floating low.

They can't walk on land, must push themselves forward, breast-first,
with their rotary feet. I wish I could photograph that.

Some kind of hawk wheels in the sky.

Under a log an orange-striped salamander wriggles like a question mark.

Moratorium on them as bait, a friend of mine once declared,
when he hooked one through the back and swore it frowned.

In the women's outhouse (why? why?) a grass spider has made a web
using the cardboard paper tube as a frame
for her own silk brand of architecture—tunnel and porch looking out

over webbing like skin stretched between large fingers,
white or evanescent depending on the angle
of light. I throw an ant on her floating mattress
and watch through a finely-crushed lens the attack.
But in print she's nearly absent, a speck: paper and lock,
plywood wall, but nothing alive. When I pick up the telephone

there are three audible clicks, followed by a dial tone to awaken the dead.

The smell in the woods today is what, *Fall Oak Leaf?*

I open a Pepsi. But there's something else . . .
I look around. Not twenty yards away sits a great gray owl, large as a child.
And she watches me like one.

Child with a thousand-year-old brain. The bird blinks,
unconcerned, keeper of a phone booth, two outhouses.
On the print, barely visible, are its eyes. Two dial tones.

Acknowledgments

Poems in *Abrupt Rural* have appeared, often in different versions, in *American Literary Review, Center, Conduit, Passages North, Permafrost, Pleiades, Third Coast, two girls' review, Willow Springs, Jacket* and *Verse*. My thanks to the editors of these journals.

photo by David Marlatt

David Dodd Lee is the author of three books of poems, including *Arrow Pointing North* (2002) and *Downsides of Fish Culture* (1997). He is also the editor of *Shade,* a new annual anthology of poetry and fiction.

New Issues Poetry & Prose

Editor, Herbert Scott

Vito Aiuto, *Self-Portrait as Jerry Quarry*
James Armstrong, *Monument In A Summer Hat*
Claire Bateman, *Clumsy*
Michael Burkard, *Pennsylvania Collection Agency*
Christopher Bursk, *Ovid at Fifteen*
Anthony Butts, *Fifth Season*
Anthony Butts, *Little Low Heaven*
Kevin Cantwell, *Something Black in the Green Part of Your Eye*
Gladys Cardiff, *A Bare Unpainted Table*
Kevin Clark, *In the Evening of No Warning*
Cynie Cory, *American Girl*
Jim Daniels, *Night with Drive-By Shooting Stars*
Joseph Featherstone, *Brace's Cove*
Lisa Fishman, *The Deep Heart's Core Is a Suitcase*
Robert Grunst, *The Smallest Bird in North America*
Paul Guest, *The Resurrection of the Body and the Ruin of the World*
Robert Haight, *Emergences and Spinner Falls*
Mark Halperin, *Time as Distance*
Myronn Hardy, *Approaching the Center*
Brian Henry, *Graft*
Edward Haworth Hoeppner, *Rain Through High Windows*
Cynthia Hogue, *Flux*
Christine Hume, *Alaskaphrenia*
Janet Kauffman, *Rot* (fiction)
Josie Kearns, *New Numbers*
Maurice Kilwein Guevara, *Autobiography of So-and-so: Poems in Prose*
Ruth Ellen Kocher, *When the Moon Knows You're Wandering*
Ruth Ellen Kocher, *One Girl Babylon*
Gerry LaFemina, *The Window Facing Winter*
Steve Langan, *Freezing*
Lance Larsen, *Erasable Walls*
David Dodd Lee, *Abrupt Rural*
David Dodd Lee, *Downsides of Fish Culture*
M.L. Liebler, *The Moon a Box*
Deanne Lundin, *The Ginseng Hunter's Notebook*
Joy Manesiotis, *They Sing to Her Bones*
Sarah Mangold, *Household Mechanics*
Gail Martin, *The Hourglass Heart*
David Marlatt, *A Hog Slaughtering Woman*
Louise Mathias, *Lark Apprentice*
Gretchen Mattox, *Buddha Box*
Gretchen Mattox, *Goodnight Architecture*

Paula McLain, *Less of Her*
Sarah Messer, *Bandit Letters*
Malena Mörling, *Ocean Avenue*
Julie Moulds, *The Woman with a Cubed Head*
Gerald Murnane, *The Plains* (fiction)
Marsha de la O, *Black Hope*
C. Mikal Oness, *Water Becomes Bone*
Elizabeth Powell, *The Republic of Self*
Margaret Rabb, *Granite Dives*
Rebecca Reynolds, *Daughter of the Hangnail; The Bovine Two-Step*
Martha Rhodes, *Perfect Disappearance*
Beth Roberts, *Brief Moral History in Blue*
John Rybicki, *Traveling at High Speeds* (expanded second edition)
Mary Ann Samyn, *Inside the Yellow Dress*
Ever Saskya, *The Porch is a Journey Different From the House*
Mark Scott, *Tactile Values*
Martha Serpas, *Côte Blanche*
Diane Seuss-Brakeman, *It Blows You Hollow*
Elaine Sexton, *Sleuth*
Marc Sheehan, *Greatest Hits*
Sarah Jane Smith, *No Thanks—and Other Stories* (fiction)
Phillip Sterling, *Mutual Shores*
Angela Sorby, *Distance Learning*
Russell Thorburn, *Approximate Desire*
Rodney Torreson, *A Breathable Light*
Robert VanderMolen, *Breath*
Martin Walls, *Small Human Detail in Care of National Trust*
Patricia Jabbeh Wesley, *Before the Palm Could Bloom: Poems of Africa*